UNIVERSITY AND KNOWLEDGE

BY

CYRIL LOVE

COPYRIGHT©2022
CYRIL LOVE

TABLE OF CONTENT

$\mathcal{INTRODUCTION}$

University (from Latin Universitas 'a whole') is an establishment of higher (or tertiary) training and research which awards instructional tiers in numerous instructional disciplines. Universities commonly provide each undergraduate and postgraduate application. The word university springs from the Latin universitas magistrorum et scholarium, which kind of means "community of teachers and students".

The primary universities have been created in Europe with the aid of church monks. The college of Bologna (Università di Bologna), based in 1088, is the first university in the sense of:

> Being a high degree-awarding institute.

- ➢ Having independence from the ecclesiastic schools, even though performed with the aid of both clergy and non-clergy.

- ➢ The use of the phrase Universitas (which changed into coined at its basis).

- ➢ Issuing secular and non-secular tiers: grammar, rhetoric, good judgment, theology, canon law, and notarial regulation.

Definition

The unique Latin phrase Universitas refers usually to "several people associated into one frame, a society, employer, network, guild, organization, etc". Like, different guilds, they had been self-regulating and decided the qualifications of their participants.

In current usage, the phrase has come to intend "An organization of higher schooling offering lessons in particular non-vocational topics and commonly having the facility to confer levels," with the sooner emphasis on its corporate organization taken into consideration as applying historically to Medieval universities.

The original Latin word mentioned degree-awarding institutions of learning in Western and relevant Europe, wherein this way of felony company became familiar and from which the institution spread around the world.

UNIVERSITY & KNOWLEDGE

CHAPTER 1

History

The college of Bologna in Italy, founded in 1088, is typically concept to be the arena's oldest college in non-stop operation.

Instructional freedom

A crucial concept in the definition of a college is that the perception of instructional freedom. The primary documentary evidence of this comes from early in the life of the college of Bologna, which adopted an academic charter, the Constitution Habita, in 1158 or 1155, which assured the precise of a traveling scholar to unhindered passage within the hobbies of training. Nowadays that is often claimed due to the fact the starting place of "educational freedom". This is regularly now extensively regarded across the world on 18 September 1988, 430 college rectors signed the Magna Carta

Universitatum, marking the 900th anniversary of Bologna's basis. The quantity of universities signing the Magna Charta Universitatum keeps growing, drawing from all elements of the planet.

Antecedents

Moroccan higher-mastering institution Al-Qarawiyin (founded in 859 A.D.) turned into converted right into a college under the supervision of the ministry of education in 1963.

Pupils from time to time name the university of al-Qarawiyyin (call given in 1963), based as a mosque by using Fatima al-Fihri in 859, a university, even though Jacques Verger writes that that is regularly performed out of scholarly comfort.

Several students remember that al-Qarawiyyin was founded and run as a madrasa until after battle II. They date the transformation of the madrasa of al-Qarawiyyin right into a university to its current reorganization in 1963. In the wake of those reforms, al-Qarawiyyin became formally renamed the "university of Al Quaraouiyine" two years later.

Some pupils, consisting of George Makdisi, have argued that early medieval universities have been motivated by the madrasas in Al-Andalus, the Emirate of Sicily, and also the close East at some stage in the Crusades. Norman Daniel, however, perspectives this argument as overstated. Roy Lowe and Yoshihito Yasuhara have these days drawn at the nicely-documented impacts of scholarship from the Islamic global on the colleges of Western Europe to involve a reconsideration of the event of higher schooling, dodging from a priority with nearby institutional structures to a broader consideration inside a global context.

Medieval Europe

The current university is in the main thought to be a proper institution that has its foundation within the Medieval Christian subculture.

ECU pedagogy occurred for decades in cathedral faculties or monastic schools (scholae monastical), inside which monks and nuns taught training; proof of those immediate forerunners of the later college at many locations dates returned to the sixth century.

In Europe, young guys proceeded to college when they had finished their study of the trivium-the preparatory arts of grammar, rhetoric, and dialectic or logic-and the quadrivium: arithmetic, geometry, music, and astronomy.

The earliest universities had been developed beneath the aegis of the Latin Church through bull as studia generalia and perhaps from cathedral schools. It's possible, however, that the occasion of cathedral faculties into universities become quite uncommon, with the university of Paris being an exception. Later they have been also based using kings (University of Naples Federico II, Charles University in Prague, Jagiellonian University in Kraków) or municipal administrations (the University of Cologne, University of Erfurt). In the early medieval duration, most new universities had been based on pre-current colleges, commonly when those schools have been deemed to possess ended up on the whole sites of upper education. Many historians country that universities and cathedral schools were a continuation of the interest in studying promoted through The residence of a religious network. Pope became crucial in promoting and regulating the concept of recent college as his 1079 Papal Decree ordered the regulated status quo of cathedral faculties that transformed themselves into the primary European universities.

The primary universities in Europe with a variety of corporate/guild shapes had been the university of Bologna (1088), the college of Paris (c.1150, later associated with the Sorbonne), and consequently the university of Oxford (1167).

The college of Bologna started as a graduate school coaching the Ius Gentium or civil regulation of peoples which turned into in call throughout Europe for the ones protecting the right of incipient international locations in opposition to empire and church. Bologna's unique declaration to school Studiorum [clarification needed] is predicated on its autonomy, its awarding of ranges, and other structural arrangements, making it the oldest continuously working institution independent of kings, emperors, or any reasonably direct religious authority.

The traditional date of 1088, or 1087 in keeping with some, facts while Irnerius commences coaching Emperor Justinian's 6th-century codification of Justinian code, the Corpus Iuris Civilis, lately observed at Pisa. Lay college students arrived within the city from many lands getting into a settlement to realize this fact, setting up themselves into 'Nationes', divided among the Cismontanes which of the Ultramontanes.

All over Europe rulers and city governments started to make universities fulfill a European thirst for understanding, and also the perception that society could get delighted from the scholarly understanding generated from those establishments. Princes and leaders of town governments perceived the capability blessings of having a scholarly know-how increase with the power to cope with hard troubles and achieve preferred ends. The emergence of humanism turned into essential to the existing information of the viable utility of universities also because of the revival of interest in knowledge received from Hellenic language texts.

The recuperation of Aristotle's works-more than 3000 pages of it would ultimately be translated-fuelled a spirit of inquiry into herbal strategies that had already begun to emerge in the 12th century. Some pupils agree with that those works represented one of the most vital document discoveries in Western intellectual history. Richard Dales, as an example, calls the discovery of Aristotle's works "a turning factor within the records of Western concept." After Aristotle reemerged, a network of students, primarily speaking in Latin, expanded the approach and exercise of trying to reconcile the mind of Greek antiquity, and specifically thoughts associated with knowledge of the plants, with those of the church. The efforts of this "scholasticism" have been focused on making use of common sense and thoughts approximately natural

The college way of life evolved else in northern Europe than it did in the south, even though the northern (basically Germany, France, and brilliant Britain) and southern universities (generally Italy) did have several rudiments in common. Latin became the language of the college, used for all textbooks, lectures, dissensions, and examinations. Professors harangued the books of Aristotle for experience, natural gospel, and theories; at the same time Hippocrates, Galen, and Avicenna had been used for drugs. Outdoor of these similarities, tremendous differences separated north and south, primarily in difficulty rely on. Italian universities focused on regulation and drugs, at the same time as the northern universities targeted the trades and theology. There have been distinct differences inside the first-rate of instruction in those areas which had been harmonious with their attention, so scholars could travel north or south grounded on their hobbies and method. There was additionally a distinction in the types of tiers provided at those universities. English, French, and German universities typically presented bachelorette's tiers, except tiers in theology, for which the doctorate became extra commonplace. Italian universities offered primarily doctorates. The difference may be attributed to the rationale of the diploma holder after scale- within the north, the point of interest tended to be on obtaining tutoring positions, whilst in the south pupils often went on to expert positions. The structure of northern universities tended to be modeled after the machine of college governance developed at the college of Paris. Southern universities tended to be patterned after the pupil-managed model all starting at the college of Bologna. In some of the southern universities, a further difference has been mentioned between the ones of northern Italy, which accompanied the sample of Bologna as a" tone- regulating, an impartial pot of students" and people of southern Italy and Iberia, which had been" innovated by using royal and Homeric responsibility to serve the requirements of presidency."

Early ultramodern universities

The college of St Andrews, innovated in 1410, is Scotland's oldest college. During the Early ultramodern period (roughly late fifteenth century to 1800), the colleges of Europe would see an extremely good quantum of the boom, productivity, and revolutionary exploration. At the cease of the middle durations, about four hundred times after the first European college become innovated, there have been 29 universities unfolding in the course of Europe. In the 15th century, 28 new bones have been created, with any other 18 delivered between 1500 and 1625. This tempo continued until by the quit of the 18th century there were roughly 143 universities in Europe, with the loftiest attention in the German Conglomerate (34), Italian international locations (26), France (25), and Spain (23), this became near a 500 growth over the number of universities in the direction of the cease of the middle periods. This wide variety doesn't include the multitudinous universities that diminished, or institutions that intermingled with other universities at some point in this time. The identity of a university wasn't inescapably egregious for the duration of the Early ultramodern length, because the period is carried out to a burgeoning quantity of establishments. In reality, the period" college" wasn't usually used to designate an advanced schooling organization. In Mediterranean countries, the term studium generale changed into nevertheless often used, at the same time as" Academy" become commonplace in Northern ECU international locations.

The propagation of universities wasn't inescapably a constant development, because the 17th century became replete with events that negatively affected college enlargement. Several wars, and in particular the Thirty instances' struggle, disintegrated the university geography in the course of Europe at distinctive times. Struggle, pest, shortage, regicide, and changes in spiritual energy and shape frequently negatively affected the societies that surpassed the guide for universities. Internal strife in the universities themselves, similar to student brawling and absentee professors, acted to destabilize those establishments as properly. Universities had been also reticent to surrender elderly lessons, and the continuing reliance on the workshop of Aristotle defied present-day advancements in awareness and the trades. This era was also suffering from the rise of the state country. As universities decreasingly got here below state manipulate, or shaped below the aegis of the state, the school governance version (which began by using the University of Paris) became increasingly more prominent. Although the elderly student-managed universities still become, they sluggishly started to move in the direction of this structural affiliation. Manipulation of universities still tended to be unbiased, even though college management turned into decreasingly appointed by using the nation.

Even though the structural model exceeded using the university of Paris, where pupil participants are managed by way of faculty" masters", surpassed a preferred for universities, the operation of this model took at least 3 one-of-a-kind bureaucracy. Some universities had a gadget of faculties whose tutoring addressed a usually unique elegance; this model tended to educate experts. There has been a collegiate or academic model grounded on the device at the college of Oxford in which tutoring and affiliation become decentralized and information changed into similarly of a generalist nature. There had been also universities that mixed those models, the usage of the collegiate model but having a centralized association.

Early ultramodern universities initially continued the class and exploration of the middle durations

- ➢ Natural Gospel,

- ➢ Feel,

- ➢ Drug,

- ➢ Theology,

- ➢ Arithmetic,

- ➢ Astronomy,

- ➢ Divination,

- ➢ Law,

- ➢ Alphabet and

- ➢ Rhetoric.

Aristotle was present-day during the magnificence, while drugs additionally depended on Galen and Arabic training. The significance of humanism for changing this country- of- affairs cannot be undervalued. Previously humanist professors joined the college, they started to transfigure the examination of the alphabet and rhetoric thru the studia humanitatis. Humanist professors focused on the capability of scholars to put in writing and communicate with distinction, to restate and interpret classical textbooks, and to live honorable lives. Other students inside the college have been tormented by the humanist techniques to literacy and their verbal moxie about historic textbooks, as well as the testimony that supported the closing significance of these textbooks. Professors of drugs comparable as Niccolò Leoniceno, Thomas Linacre, and William Cop have been frequently skilled in and tutored from a humanist angle in addition to restated vital ancient medical textbooks. The important attitude communicated using humanism becomes imperative for modifications in universities and training. For case, Andreas Vesalius become educated in a humanist style earlier than producing a restatement of Galen, whose ideas he vindicated thru his very own deconstructions. In law, Andreas Alciatus invested the Corpus Juris with a humanist attitude, while Jacques Cujas's humanist jottings have been consummate to his individual as a Justice of the Peace. Philipp Melanchthon noted the workshop of Erasmus as an in large part influential associate for connecting theology back to original textbooks, which became vital for the reform at Protestant universities. Galileo Galilei, who tutored at the colleges of Pisa and Padua, and Martin Luther, who tutored at the college of Wittenberg (as did Melanchthon), additionally had humanist training. The assignment of the humanists turned into to sluggishly percolate the college; to growth the humanist presence in professorships and chairpersons, syllabi, and handbooks so that posted workshops would show the humanistic ideal of know-how and universities.

Even though the original focus of the humanist pupils inside the college turned into the discovery, exposition, and insertion of ancient textbooks and languages into the university, the ideas of those textbooks on society usually, affect on became finally exceedingly innovative. The emergence of classical textbooks added new ideas and led to a further innovative college climate (as the notable list of scholars above attests to). A focus on know-how coming from tone, from the mortal, has direct recrimination for brand new sorts of training and practice, and become the inspiration for what's generally referred to as the arts. This disposition closer to knowledge manifested in no longer without a doubt the restatement and propagation of historic textbooks, but also their adaption and growth. For case, Vesalius was imperative for championing the usage of Galen, however, he additionally amped this textbook with the trial, dissensions, and further exploration. The propagation of those textbooks, especially in the universities, changed into greatly sponsored via the emergence of the printing press and the morning of the use of the conversational, which allowed for the printing of fairly large textbooks at reasonable fees.

Inspecting the influence of humanism on scholars in drugs, arithmetic, astronomy, and capsules can also advise that humanism and universities have been a sturdy motivation for the scientific revolution. Even though the relationship between humanism and clinical discovery may additionally assuredly properly have begun in the confines of the university, the relationship has been usually perceived as having been disassociated via the changing nature of know-how throughout the Scientific Revolution. Chroniclers are comparable to Richards. Westfall has argued that the overt conservatism of universities inhibited attempts tore-conceptualize nature and understanding and brought on an unforgettable pressure between universities and scientists. This resistance to modifications in knowledge may also have been a substantial thing in riding numerous scientists down from the college and toward personal donors, commonly in kingly courts, and institutions with these days forming medical societies.

Other chroniclers discover a contradiction in the proposition that the very place in which the tremendous wide variety of the scholars that instructed the medical revolution entered their training should additionally be the area that inhibits their exploration and the advancement of awareness. In truth, in addition, 80 of the EU scientists between 1450 and 1650 protected within the Dictionary of clinical memoir had been college skilled, of which roughly 45 held university posts. It becomes the case that the instructional foundations remaining from the center intervals had been stable, and they did give for a terrain that fostered extensive boom and improvement. There was a giant disinclination on the part of universities to relinquish the concord and comprehensiveness handed with the aid of the Aristotelian device, which became effective as a coherent device for knowledge and decoding the sector. Still, university professors nonetheless hired some autonomy, as a minimum inside the lores, to pick out epistemological foundations and styles. For case, Melanchthon and his votaries at the college of Wittenberg have been necessary for integrating Copernican great constructs into astronomical debate and education. Any other illustration becomes the quick-lived however pretty rapid-fireplace relinquishment of Cartesian epistemology and method in EU universities, and the debates girding that relinquishment, which led to further mechanistic strategies to medical troubles in addition to establishing an openness to trade. Various exemplifications belie the usually perceived mulishness of universities. Although universities may have been slow to accept new lores and methodologies as they surfaced, once they did accept new thoughts it helped to bring legality and respectability, and supported the scientific modifications thru furnishing a stable terrain for coaching and cloth coffers.

Anyhow of the manner the strain among universities, character scientists, and the clinical revolution itself is perceived, there was a perceptible effect on the way that university educations become built. Aristotelian epistemology handed a coherent frame no longer actually for knowledge and expertise production, but additionally for the training of scholars inside the advanced education placing. The introduction of the latest clinical constructs throughout the medical revolution, and the epistemological challenges that had been crucial within this creation initiated

The idea of each autonomy of information and the dimensions of the disciplines. As a substitute for getting into advanced schooling to come a" general scholar" immersed in getting complete inside the whole magnificence, there surfaced a sort of pupil that positioned wisdom first and viewed it as a vocation in itself. The divergence among the ones focused on wisdom and people nonetheless rooted within the idea of a well-known scholar aggravated the epistemological pressures that have been formerly starting to crop.

The epistemological pressures between scientists and universities have been also heightened by using the profitable realities of exploration in the course of this time, as character scientists, associations, and universities had been fighting for confined coffers. There was also opposition from the conformation of recent sodalities funded using private donors and designed to offer free training to the general public, or installed using authentic governments to present a knowledge-empty crowd with volition to standard universities. Indeed whilst universities supported new clinical trials, and the university handed foundational education and authority for the exploration and conclusions, they couldn't contend with the coffers to be had through private donors.

Using the stop of the early ultramodern length, the shape and exposure of advanced education had been modified in ways that might be eminently recognizable for the ultramodern environment. Aristotle became not a force furnishing the epistemological and methodological consciousness for universities and greater mechanistic publicity was bobbing up. The hierarchical area of theological information had for the maximum component been displaced and the humanities had come into a group, and a new openness was starting to take hold inside the construction and dispersion of expertise that has been to come back vital for the conformation of the ultramodern country.

Ultramodern universities

King's university London, established by the Royal constitution having been innovated by way of King George IV and Duke of Wellington in 1829, is one of the founding sodalities of the college of London.

Ultramodern universities constitute a council or quasi-guild system. This hand of the college gadget failed to trade because of its supplemental standing in an industrialized frugality; as commerce evolved between municipalities in Europe at some point of the center durations, though different orders stood within the manner of growing commerce and thus have been in the end abolished, the scholar's council did now not. In keeping with annalist Elliot Krause, "The College and scholars' orders held onto their strength over elegance, schooling, and plant because early capitalism wasn't interested in it."

By the 18th century, universities posted their very own exploration journals and by the nineteenth century, the German and the French university models had arisen. The German, or Humboldtian model, was conceived with the aid of Wilhelm von Humboldt and grounded on Friedrich Schleiermacher's liberal thoughts referring to the significance of freedom, forums, and laboratories in universities. The French college model involved strict areas and control over each component of the university.

Till the nineteenth century, faith played a huge element in university class; nevertheless, the part of religion in exploration universities dropped throughout that century. Using the give-up of the nineteenth century, the German college version had to unfold around the world. Universities focused on wisdom in the 19th and 20th centuries and came in decreasingly handy to the tens of millions. Within America, Johns Hopkins College changed into the primary to borrow the (German) exploration college version and innovated the relinquishment of that version by using utmost American universities. When Johns Hopkins became innovated in 1876," nearly the whole college had studied in Germany. The British also installed universities international and superior training came to be had to the tens of millions now not handiest in Europe.

In 1963, Robbin's document on universities within the UK concluded that similar institutions have to have four primary" objects important to any duly balanced system instruction in chops; the creation of the overall powers of the mind to produce no longer naked professionals but rather cultivated men and women; to hold exploration in balance with tutoring, seeing that tutoring shouldn't be separated from the advancement of literacy and the quest for verity; and to transmit a common subculture and not unusual norms of citizenship."

Inside the early twenty-first century, organizations were raised over the adding materialization and standardization of universities worldwide. Neo-liberal operation models have on this feel been critiqued for creating" industrial universities (in which) energy is transferred from college to directors, profitable apologies dominate, and the familiar nethermost line' eclipses pedagogical or intellectual companies". Lecturers' know-how of time, pedagogical pride, vocation, and collegiality has been mentioned as viable ways of easing comparable issues.

Public universities

A public university is normally a university created or run by using a public nation however at an equal time represents a nation's autonomic institution which functions as an independent body interior of the same kingdom. A few public universities are almost associated with public creative, nonsecular or political bournes, for case the countrywide university of eire, which shaped incompletely from the

Catholic college of Eire which becomes created nearly incontinently and mainly in solution to the non-denominational universities which had been set up in Eire in 1850. Inside the instances leading up to the Easter growing, and in no small part a result of the Gaelic Romantic revivalists, the NUI accumulated a large quantum of records on the Irish language and Irish subculture. Reforms in Argentina had been the result of the university Revolution of 1918 and its posterior reforms with the aid of incorporating values that sought for a greater same and laic superior schooling gadget.

Intergovernmental universities

Universities created with the aid of bilateral or multinational covenants among nations are intergovernmental. An illustration is the Academy of European law, which gives education in European regulation to legal professionals, judges, barristers, solicitors, in-house counsel, and academics. EUCLID (Pôle Universitaire Euclide, Euclid College) is chartered as a college and marquee association dedicated to sustainable improvement in signatory nations, and the united international locations college engages in sweats to solve the pressing global troubles which can be of problem to the

United countries, its peoples and member countries. The European University Institute, a post-graduate university specializing in social life, is formally an intergovernmental affiliation, installed with the aid of the member countries of the ECU Union.

CHAPTER 2

Organization

Even though each group is organized else, almost all universities have a board of trustees; a boss, chancellor, or rector; as a minimum one vice president, vice-chancellor, or vice-rector; and elders of colorful divisions. Universities are usually divided into several educational departments, seminaries, or colleges. Public university structures are dominated by way of government-run superior schooling forums. They overview economic requests and financial proffers and additionally allocate price range for every college in the gadget. They also authorize new applications of practice and cancel or make modifications to being applications. Further, they plan for the further coordinated increase and improvement of the colorful institutions of superior education in the state or us of a. Nevertheless, several public universities in the international have a vast degree of financial, exploration, and pedagogical autonomy. Private universities are in detail funded and usually have broader independence from national packages. Nevertheless, they may have decreased independence from commercial enterprise pots depending on the source of their finances.

Around the arena

The backing and association of universities vary substantially between specific countries around the world. In some international locations, universities are commonly funded by using the kingdom, while in others backing might also come from benefactors or from freights which scholars attending the university have to pay. In a few countries, the good sized adulthood of scholars attend the university of their authentic town, whilst in different countries, universities appeal to pupils from all over the arena and can give university lodging for or her students.

Bracket

The outline of a college varies notably, certainly within a few nations. Where there is clarification, it's commonly set by using a government organization. For instance

In Australia, the Tertiary education first-class and norms company (TEQSA) is Australia's impartial public controller of the superior education sector. Scholars' rights within the college are also defended by the education services for distant places Students Act (ESOS).

Inside the United States, there may be no nationally standardized description for the term university, even though the term has traditionally been used to designate exploration institutions and was previously reserved for doctorate-granting exploration establishments. Some nations, similar to Massachusetts, will only grant an academy" college fame" if it grants at the least doctoral stages.

In the UK, the Privy Council is answerable for approving the usage of the phrase university inside the call of an organization, underneath the phrases of the farther and superior schooling Act 1992.

In India, a brand new designation supposed universities have been created for universities of the superior education that isn't universities, however, work at a usually excessive general in a particular location. Establishments that might be intended- to-be-university' revel in the educational fame and the boons of a university. Via this provision, numerous seminaries which might be marketable and were installed simply to take advantage of the demand for superior training have sprung up.

In Canada, the council commonly refers to a - time,non-diploma-granting institution, at the same time as college connotes a four-time, degree-granting institution. Universities may also be sub-labeled (as within the Macleans ratings) into huge exploration universities with numerous Ph.D. granting packages and scientific seminaries (for instance, McGill university);" comprehensive" universities which have a few PhDs but aren't geared in the direction of exploration (comparable as Waterloo); and decrease, frequently undergraduate universities (similar as St. Francis Xavier).

In Germany, universities are institutions of advanced training that have the electricity to confer bachelorette, grasp, and Ph.D. ranges. They're explicitly regarded as comparable via regulation and cannot be innovated without authorities' blessing. The term Universität (i.e. The German term for college) is defended through regulation and any use without a sanctioned blessing is a felonious offense. Utmost of them are public institutions, though many private universities live. Comparable universities are usually exploration universities. Piecemeal from these universities, Germany has other institutions of superior training (Hochschule, Fachhochschule). Fachhochschule way an advanced schooling organization that has similarities to the former polytechnics in the British training gadget, the English period used for these German institutions is common' university of carried out lores'. They could confer grasp's tiers however no PhDs. They're analogous to the version of tutoring universities with lower exploration and the exploration prevalent being largely realistic Hochschule can relate to colorful styles of institutions, regularly specialized in a sure field (e.g. Track, high-quality trades, enterprise). They could or may not have the strength to award Ph.D. tiers, relying on the separate government legislation. But, their rank is considered unique to that of universities right (Universität), if not, if they award Ph.D. degrees.

UNIVERSITY & KNOWLEDGE

CHAPTER 3

Knowledge

Knowledge is familiarity or mindfulness, of someone or commodity, similar to records (descriptive expertise), chops (procedural know-how), or objects (familiarity expertise), regularly contributing to understanding. Knowledge of statistics, additionally appertained to as propositional knowledge, is often described as a proper notion that is awesome from opinion or guesswork via distinctive features of defense. At the same time as there's extensive agreement amongst proponents that it's a shape of real perception, numerous problems in gospel consciousness on defense whether it's demanded at every, how to apprehend it, and whether or not commodity otherwise except it is demanded. These problems were boosted due to a series of looks at trials by Edmund Gettier and have provoked colorful vital delineations. Some of them deny that protection is necessary and replace it, for instance, with trustability or the incarnation of cognitive deserves. Others contend that protection is demanded but formulate fresh situations, for instance, that no defeaters of the belief are present or that the person could now not have the perception if it changed into false.

The owl of Athena is an image of knowledge

Knowledge can be produced through several specific approaches. The most vital supply is perception, which refers to the operation of the five senses. Numerous proponents additionally include soul-searching as a supply of information, no longer of external physical items, but 1's inner countries. Other resources frequently bandied include memory, rational suspicion, conclusion, and evidence. In line with foundationalism, a number of those sources are introductory in the experience that they can justify beliefs without depending on other internal nations. This declaration is rejected by coherentists, who contend that a sufficient diploma of consonance among all of the inner international locations of the religionist is necessary for knowledge.

Numerous distinctive elements of understanding are delved and it performs an element in colorful disciplines. It is the number one difficulty of the sector of epistemology, which studies what we know, how we come to realize it, and what it approaches to recognize commodity. The problem of the cost of information enterprises is the question of why expertise is more precious than bare actual perception. Philosophical dubitation is the debatable thesis that we warrant any shape of know-how or that information is insolvable. Formal epistemology research, among different consequences, the policies governing how know-how and affiliated international locations endure, and in what relations they stand to every different?. Science tries to gather an understanding of the usage of the medical system, that's grounded on unremarkable trials, statements, and measurements. Numerous persuasions preserve that human beings need to search for expertise and that God or the godly is the source of know-how.

Delineations

Multitudinous delineations of understanding had been suggested. The expressions" generality of knowledge"," proposition of knowledge", and" evaluation of understanding" are sometimes hired as antonyms. There may be a huge, even though not commonplace, settlement among proponents that know-how may be characterized as a cognitive achievement or an epistemic contact with reality and that propositional understanding is a shape of proper perception. Utmost delineations of understanding in logical gospel cease to determine the important features of propositional expertise, which is likewise appertained to as information- that. Understanding- that may be expressed using that- clauses as in" I realize that Dave is at home". It contrasts with knowledge- style (recognize- how) expressing realistic capability, as in" she knows a way to swim", and knowledge with the aid of familiarity, which refers to a familiarity with the given item grounded on former direct experience.

There is numerous deep dissensions approximately know-how's specific nature despite settlement on those fashionable but indistinct characteristics. One description that several proponents recall being preferred is justified true belief (JTB).

Still, it has been blamed on special approaches and numerous crucial delineations were advised. These dissensions have colorful assets that belong to the pretensions and patterns inside epistemology and different fields, or to variations regarding the norms of information that humans intend to uphold. A few proponents give attention to information's most salient features of their try and give a surely useful description. Others try to provide a theoretically precise description through list the situations which are together vital and concertedly enough. The term" evaluation of information" is often used for this method. It may be understood in analogy to how druggists dissect a pattern by looking for a listing of all of the chemical rudiments composing it.

Methodological differences problem whether or not experimenters predicate their inquiry on abstract and well-known anticipations or suppositions, or on concrete and precise instances, appertained to as Methodism and particularism, independently. Another source of confrontation is the part of ordinary language in one's inquiry the load is given to how the period" know-how" is utilized in every day communication. Consistent with Ludwig Wittgenstein, for illustration, there may be no clean- reduced the description of understanding because it is only a cluster of generalities associated via the circle of relatives resemblance.

Different Generalizations of the norms of information are also answerable for colorful dissensions. A few epistemologists maintain that knowledge demands usually excessive conditions, like infallibility, and is as a consequence exceedingly uncommon. Others see know-how as an alternatively commonplace miracle, modern-day in numerous everyday conditions, without exorbitantly excessive norms.

Justified real belief

Several proponents outline information as justified true belief (JTB). This description characterizes know-how through three critical capabilities as

1. It is a perception

2. Authentic and

3. Justified.

In the dialogue Theaetetus by using the historical Greek champion Plato, Socrates pondered the distinction between information and proper notion, however, rejected the JTB description of understanding. The most significantly well-known point is verity bone can believe commodity false however one cannot recognize commodity fake. Many regular language proponents have raised dubieties that expertise is a shape of notion grounded on everyday expressions like" I do not consider that; I understand it". Utmost proponents reject this difference and explain similar expressions via the inscrutability of natural language. The principle contestation girding the JTB description concerns its third-factor defense. The provocation for together with this detail is that several real beliefs do supposedly now not quantity to know-how. Specifically, this covers cases of superstition, fortunate suppositions, or incorrect common sense. The corresponding ideals might also indeed be genuine but it seems there may be in addition to expertise than just being proper approximate commodity. The JTB description solves this problem by relating proper protection because the sparkling element demanded, is absent within the beneath-cited instances. Numerous proponents have understood defense internalistically (internalism) is a notion that is justified if it is supported by way of another internal country of the man or woman, similar to a perceptual revel in, a memory, or an exchange perception. This inner country has to constitute a sufficiently sturdy substantiation or cause for the believed proposition. A few ultramodern performances alter the JTB description by using an externalist generality of defense instead. This defense depends not simply on elements inner to the situation but additionally on external elements. They could encompass, for example, that the belief changed into produced via a dependable manner or that the believed fact precipitated the perception.

Gettier trouble and druthers

The JTB description came beneath extreme review inside the 20th century, while Edmund Gettier gave a sequence of counterexamples. They purport to present concrete cases of justified real beliefs that fail to represent expertise. The purpose for his or her failure is normally a shape of epistemic success the defense does not apply to the verity. In a well-recognized illustration, there is a rustic street with numerous barn facades and only one actual barn. The individual driving is not anxious about this, stops by a lucky coexistence in the front of the real barn, and forms the notion that he's in the front of a barn. It's been argued that this justified genuine belief would not constitute knowledge for the reason that an individual would not have been appropriate to tell the distinction without the fortuitous twist of fate. So indeed though the perception is justified, it is a lucky coexistence that it's also text the responses to these counterexamples had been exceptional. In keeping with a few, they display that the JTB description of understanding is deeply faulty and that a thorough reconceptualization of understanding is necessary, often using denying defense a component. This will be, for example, with the aid of replacing protection with trustability or by using information know-how as the incarnation of cognitive deserves. Other strategies encompass defining it regarding the cognitive part it plays in furnishing motives for doing or allowing commodity or seeing it as the most standard factive internal nation motive force. Colorful proponents are diametrically against the novel reconceptualization and both deny that Gettier cases pose issues or they are trying to interrupt them by using making decreased variations to how the defense is described. Similar approaches affect on a minimal revision of the JTB description.

Among those axes, a few proponents have recommended colorful mild departures. They agree that the JTB description is a step in the proper direction justified real belief is a necessary circumstance of knowledge. Nonetheless, they differ in that it's a sufficient condition. They preserve instead that a clean criterion, some point X, is necessary for know-how. For this reason, they're regularly appertained to as JTB X delineations of information. A nearly affiliated technique speaks now not of protection but of going away and defines go away as protection collectively with something otherwise is essential to arrive at understanding. Several campaigners for the fourth factor have been counseled. In this regard, expertise can be defined as the justified real belief that does not rely on any fake ideals, that there are no defeaters present, or that the person might not have the belief if it became false. According to Simon Blackburn, those who have a justified real notion' thru a disfigurement, excrescence, or failure' fail to know. Similar and analogous delineations are a success at avoiding numerous of the unique Gettier instances. Nonetheless, they frequently fall prey to recently conceived counterexamples. To keep away from all feasible instances, it may be necessary to find a criterion that excludes all types of epistemic good fortune. It's been argued that this type of criterion would set the wanted norms of knowledge usually grandly the perception must be unerring to reach all cases. This would imply that veritably a lot of our beliefs quantum to expertise if any. For example, Richard Kirkham suggests that our description of knowledge calls for the substantiation for the belief necessitates its verity. There's still veritably little settlement within the academic communication as to which of the proposed variations or reconceptualizations is correct.

Types

The English word information can restate an expansion of words in other languages that relate to exclusive countries. The Latin words cognition and Scientia can both be restated as" expertise". Love languages have two principal verbs that might both be restated as" to understand" for instance, connaître and savoir in French or conocer and smallsword in Spanish. In historical Greek, there have been four comparable important knowledge phrases epistēmē (unchanging theoretical expertise), technē (expert specialized know-how), mētis (strategic expertise), and gnōsis (unique intellectual expertise). Most of these special forms of know-how may be considered forms of cognitive success.

Propositional knowledge

Propositional knowledge, also appertained to as descriptive know-how, is the conventional sort of understanding in the logical gospel, and colorful corporations are used to differentiate among its one-of-a-kind subtypes. The differences among the essential types are normally drawn grounded on the verbal phrasings used to express them. Propositional expertise is propositional within the sense that it entails a relation to a proposition. Because propositions are often expressed through that- clauses, it's also appertained to as information- that, as in" Akari is aware that Canberra is the capital of Australia". In this example, Akari stands inside the relation of understanding to the proposition" Canberra is the capital of Australia". Nearly affiliated kinds of knowledge are know-how, for illustration, understanding which the Taj Mahal is or knowing who killed J.F. Kennedy. Those expressions are usually understood as sorts of propositional knowledge seeing that they usually can be reworded with the use of that clause.

A crucial distinction amongst propositional forms of expertise is between apriori and aposteriori understanding. For aposteriori knowledge, its protection is grounded on empirical substantiation, like sensitive experience. It contrasts with apriori information, that's grounded on the pure cause or rational suspicion without the want for sensation. Apriori know-how is on occasion connected with ingrain knowledge that is inborn and would not want to be lately discovered. A popular suggestion for these types encompasses the expertise of introductory satisfactory claims, like" $2+2 = 4$". It's outstanding from acquired understanding, which the man or woman wishes to analyze first to preserve it. Nearly affiliated differences are those among essential and contingent understanding, grounded on whether or not it's viable in any respect that the known proposition is fake, as well as among logical and artificial knowledge, grounded on whether the verity of the known proposition relies upon handiest at the meaning of the phrases it uses.

A distinctive distinction is that between occurrence and dispositional information. It glasses the difference between occurrence and dispositional beliefs to understand currently way to entertain the corresponding representation currently, to be nervous of it." Dispositional understanding" refers back to the bare functionality to accomplish that without its prosecution. In this regard, a person completely immersed in a pass-kart race has dispositional however, not occurrence understanding of where their domestic is. The reason is that they're presently enthralled with commodities otherwise however could fluently supply these statistics if they stopped and concentrated on it.

Non-propositional knowledge

For-propositional understanding, no critical relation to a proposition is concerned. The 2 maximum well-recognized paperwork is expertise- style (recognize- how or procedural know-how) and information by familiarity. The term" know-how" refers to a few shapes of realistic capability or talent. It can be defined as having the corresponding functionality. Exemplifications include knowing a way to trip a motorbike or knowing a way to play the guitar. Some of the capacities accountable for realizing- fashion may additionally contain positive types of information- that, such as understanding the way to prove an exceptional theorem. However, this is not typically the case. It is usually argued that considerably people and possibly other advanced creatures maintain propositional knowledge since it requires a complicated shape of thoughts. Sensible knowledge, alternatively, is greater commonplace inside the beast's vicinity. In this regard, an ant knows how to walk indeed even though it presumably lacks a mind sufficiently developed enough to stand in a relation to the corresponding proposition by representing it.

Information via familiarity refers to familiarity with an existent that effect from direct existential contact with this existent. Its often, but not truly, issues relation to someone. On the verbal position, it would not endure that- clause and may be expressed using an immediate object. So while a person claims that they realize Wladimir Klitschko's tête-à-tête, they may be expressing that they had a certain type of touch with him and not that they recognize a certain reality about him. This is normally understood to mean that it constitutes a relation to a concrete existent and now not to a proposition. Information with the aid of familiarity plays a primary part in Bertrand Russell's epistemology. He contrasts it with know-how by description, which is a form of propositional expertise not grounded on direct perceptual experience. So by using watching a talkie about Wladimir Klitschko, the bystander can also accumulate colorful kinds of knowledge via description approximately him, for example, approximately his country or his career in boxing, without obtaining understanding with the aid of familiarity of him. Still, there may be some contestation about whether it's feasible to acquire information with the aid of familiarity in its pure-propositional form. In this regard, some proponents have advised that it is probably better to understand it as one form of propositional understanding it is simplest expressed in a grammatically exclusive manner.

CHAPTER 4

Other Differences

Tone- know-how

Tone-knowledge, generally refers to a person's expertise in their very own sensations, research, ideals, and different internal nations. Several questions concerning tone-expertise was the issue of expansive debates in the gospel, along with whether tone-expertise differs from other kinds of understanding, whether we've privileged tone-expertise as compared to information of different minds, and the nature of our familiarity with ourselves. David Hume expressed dubitation about whether or not we may want to ever have tone- understanding over and above our instantaneous mindfulness of a" P.C.

Placed expertise

Positioned know-how is expertise unique to a specific state of affairs. It become utilized by Donna Haraway as an extension of the feminist methods of" successor wisdom" recommended by Sandra Harding, one which" offers a extra appropriate, richer, better account of a global, that allows you to stay in it properly and in vital, reflexive relation to our very own in addition to others' practices of domination and the unstable hall of honor and oppression that makes up all positions." this situation incompletely transforms know-how into a story, which Arturo Escobar explains as," neither inventions nor supposed facts." This narrative of situation is literal textures woven of fact and fabrication, and as Escobar explains in addition," certainly the maximum impartial scientific disciplines are narratives on this feel," averring that in preference to a cause brushing off knowledge as a trivial be counted of contingency," it's miles to deal with (this narrative) in the most severe way, without succumbing to its mystification as' the verity' or to the ironic dubitation not unusual to numerous critiques."

Haraway's argument stems from the restrictions of the mortal belief, as well as the overemphasis on the experience of vision in wisdom. According to Haraway, imaginative and prescient knowledge have been," used to signify a vault out of the mentioned body and right into a conquering thing from nowhere. This causes an issue of perspectives in the position of know-how itself as an implicit participant in the creation of information, performing in a role of" modest substantiation". This is what Haraway terms a" god trick", or the forenamed representation while escaping illustration. So that it will avoid this," Haraway perpetuates a subculture of observation which emphasizes the significance of the issue in terms of each ethical and political responsibility".

A few forms of producing understanding, similar to trial and mistake, or gaining knowledge from enjoyment, generally tend to produce in large part situational information. Situational knowledge is often bedded in language, subculture, or traditions. This integration of situational information is an allusion to the network, and its tries at gathering non-public views into a personification" of views from almost." information are likewise said to be related to the capacity of acknowledgment in mortal beings.

Certainly, even though Haraway's arguments are in large part grounded on feminist studies, this idea of various worlds, in addition to the unbeliever station of located information is present within the important arguments of post-structuralism. Unnaturally, both argue the contingency of expertise on the presence of records; power, and terrain, as well as the rejection of commonplace rules or laws or abecedarian systems; and the idea of energy as an inherited particularity of incorporation.

Advanced and lower knowledge

Numerous forms of Eastern Church and religion distinguish between advanced and lower knowledge. They're also appertained to as para vidya and para vidya in Hinduism or the two trueness doctrine in Buddhism. Lower knowledge is grounded on the senses and the intellect. In this regard, all forms of empirical and objective knowledge belong to this order. utmost of the knowledge demanded in one's everyday functioning is lower knowledge. It's about mundane or conventional effects that are in tune with common sense, like that mice are lower than mammoths. It applies to numerous practical issues, like how to repair an auto or how to convert a client. Scientific knowledge, for illustration, that the chemical composition of water is H2O, is frequently seen as one of the most advanced forms of lower knowledge.

Advanced knowledge, on the other hand, is understood as knowledge of God, the absolute, the true tone, or the ultimate reality. It belongs neither to the external world of physical objects nor to the internal world of the experience of feelings and generalities. Numerous spiritual training emphasizes the increased significance, or occasionally indeed exclusive significance, of advanced knowledge in comparison to lower knowledge. This is generally grounded on the idea that achieving advanced knowledge is one of the central ways on the spiritual path. In this regard, advanced knowledge is seen as what frees the existent from ignorance, helps them realize God, or liberates them from the cycle of revitalization. This is frequently combined with the view that lower knowledge is in some way grounded on a vision it belongs to the realm of bare appearances or Maya, while advanced knowledge manages to view the reality underpinning these appearances. In the Buddhist tradition, the attainment of advanced knowledge or ultimate verity is frequently associated with seeing the world from the perspective of sunyata, i.e. as a form of emptiness lacking essential actuality or Sources of knowledge

Sources of knowledge are ways how people come to know effects or how knowledge is created. Different sources of knowledge are bandied in the academic literature, frequently in terms of the internal faculties responsible. They include perception, soul-searching, memory, conclusion, and evidence. Still, not everyone agrees that all of them lead to knowledge. Generally, perception or observation, i.e. using one of the five senses, is linked as the most important source. So knowing that the baby is sleeping constitutes experimental knowledge if it was caused by a perception of the snoring baby. But this would not be the case if one learned about this fact through a telephone discussion with one's partner. Direct realists explain experimental knowledge by holding that perception constitutes direct contact with the perceived object. Circular realists, on the other hand, contend that this contact happens laterally we can only directly perceive sense data, which are also interpreted as representing external objects. This distinction is important since it affects whether the knowledge of external objects is direct or circular and may therefore have an impact on how certain the knowledge is.

Soul-searching is frequently seen in analogy to perception as a source of knowledge, not of external physical objects, but internal countries. Traditionally, colorful proponents have credited a special epistemic status to soul-searching by claiming that it's unerring or that there's no introspective difference between appearance and reality. Still, this claim has been queried in the contemporary converse. Critics argue that it may be possible, for illustration, to mistake an unwelcome itch for pain or to confuse the experience of a slight cirque for the experience of a circle. Perceptual and introspective knowledge frequently act as a form of abecedarian or introductory knowledge. According to some researchers, perceptual knowledge is the only source of introductory knowledge and provides the foundation for all other knowledge.

Reminiscence is generally diagnosed as any other source of knowledge. It differs from belief and introspection in that it is not as independent or fundamental as they're since it relies upon other preceding studies. The school of reminiscence keeps understanding received inside the beyond and makes it accessible within the present, as when remembering a beyond occasion or a friend's phone wide variety. It is usually taken into consideration a reliable supply of understanding, however, it can mislead us at times although, and either due to the fact the unique revel in changed into unreliable or because the memory degraded and does now not as it should represent the original revel in anymore.

Information primarily based on belief, introspection, or memory may additionally supply an upward push to inferential expertise, which comes approximately when reasoning is implemented to draw inferences from every other recognized reality. In this regard, the perceptual expertise of a Czech stamp on a postcard may also give an upward thrust to the inferential know-how that one's friend is touring the Czech Republic. In keeping with rationalists, a few types of information are completely unbiased of observation and introspection. They had to explain how sure apriori beliefs, just like the mathematical notion that $2 + 2 = 4$, constitute know-how. Some theorists keep that the faculty of natural cause or rational instinct is responsible in those instances because there appear to be no sensory perceptions that would justify such widespread and abstract understanding. However, difficulties in providing a clear account of pure purpose or rational intuition have led numerous empirically minded epistemologists to doubt that they constitute impartial assets of understanding. An intently associated approach is to hold that this type of knowledge is innate. In keeping with Plato's theory of recollection, as an example, it is accessed via a special shape of remembering.

UNIVERSITY & KNOWLEDGE

CHAPTER 5

Structure of knowledge

The expression "structure of understanding" refers back to the way wherein the mental states of a person need to be related to every other for information to get up. Most theorists preserve that, amongst different things, an agent has to have proper motives for containing a belief if this perception is to quantity to knowledge. So whilst challenged, the agent may additionally justify their notion with the aid of relating to their motive for containing it. In lots of cases, this cause is itself a notion that can as nicely be challenged. So while the agent believes that Ford vehicles are more inexpensive than BMWs because they trust to have heard this from a reliable supply, they will be challenged to justify why they accept as true that their supply is reliable. If it seems that their motives aren't well supported, this also affects the epistemic reputation of the authentic belief. But, something aid their gift can also be challenged. This threatens to lead to an infinite regress because the epistemic reputation at every step relies upon the epistemic reputation of the preceding step. Theories of the shapes of knowledge respond to a way on how to solve this trouble.

The three maximum commonplace theories are foundationalism, coherentism, and infinitism. Foundationalists and coherentists deny the life of this countless regress, in contrast to infinities. In step with foundationalists, some fundamental reasons have their epistemic repute impartial to other reasons and thereby represent the endpoint of the regress. Towards this view, it has been argued that the idea of "basic motive" is contradictory: there needs to be a purpose for why some motives are basic and others are non-basic, in which case the fundamental reasons might rely upon any other purpose despite everything and would therefore no longer be fundamental. An additional hassle is composed of finding manageable candidates for simple motives.

Coherentists and infinities keep away from those troubles by denying the difference between primary and non-primary reasons. Coherentists argue that there may be simplest a finite wide variety of motives, which jointly support every other and thereby ensure every other's epistemic status. As an example, if perception b1 supports perception b2 and belief b2 supports belief b1, the agent has a reason for accepting one belief if they have already got the alternative. However, their mutual help by me isn't always an excellent motive for newly accepting both ideals straight away. A closely associated issue is that there may be various distinct units of coherent ideals and coherentists face the problem of explaining why we should be given one coherent set in place of another. For infinities, in the evaluation of foundationalists and coherentists, there may be a limitless quantity of motives. This position faces the trouble of explaining how human understanding is possible at all since it appears that the human mind is limited and cannot own a countless quantity of motives. Of their conventional paperwork, foundationalists, coherentists, and infinities all face the Gettier trouble, a thing of financial growth. Over time, researchers have emphasized the significance of better education in human capital formation and monetary boom. As an example, there is research that has shown that there's a more suggested boom in nations wherein it is properly evolved the system of higher training. Past the various research and models built over time that allows you to exhibit the connection between schooling and competitiveness, it's miles apparent that its position has been diagnosed additionally via global bodies worried with measuring the monetary competitiveness of nations and their ranking according to degree and its dynamics. There are international businesses with preoccupations in this area: the sector economic discussion board (global economic discussion board-WEF), which published starting in 1979 The file on international Competitiveness, and the Institute for control and development global Institute for

1. Loss of schooling in this subject

2. Lack of activities that sell the Romanian technical advent

3. Low interest in countrywide historical past research

4. Failing to come across the significance of innovative interest in the evolution procedure

5. Lack of helping the concept of the innovation method decreased hobby in protecting the I.P. Right.

Management development MD. The indicator of global Competitiveness (international Competitiveness Index) conducted by using the WEF in shape based totally on twelve pillars that relate to public and private establishments, infrastructure, macroeconomics, health, and primary training, better education and training, the performance of markets, labor marketplace efficiency, financial market complexity, technology, markets dimensions, business complexity, and improvements. Analyzing these pillars, we can see that schooling is reflected in many of them. Higher education can be observed in the form of various indicators, both without delay or circuitously, within the case of signs' "public and personal establishments" regarding the quality of tutorial establishments and people which have a function of coverage-making and coverage implementation in the discipline and the fact that they positioned its mark on the competitiveness.

As regards the "efficiency of the labor marketplace" is clear in the fine of labor force dependency on the education machine. Inside this pillar can be discovered inclusive of the phenomenon of brain drain. If we speak of generation must be highlighted the technological capability of a country and that it's far determined by way of the excellent better training in universities. Inside the same context, the indicator associated with innovation, highlights the truth that it cannot exist without establishment of studies, the body of workers of fantastically skilled scientists and engineers, and research and improvement centers which can exploit relationships between universities and agencies, and without highbrow belongings protection.

Conclusions

The economic importance of highbrow assets is gaining popularity and interest and can't be overstated and, certainly, it is receiving a fantastic deal of interest international. To strengthen the cause of the blessings of highbrow property safety at the country-wide and international levels, training in highbrow belongings is needed and must be endorsed. We need to make people, industries, and governments privy to the concept of intellectual belongings, and handiest then can they take positions on the difficulty so one can impact trade. Inside the developing international, the question of highbrow assets and their education is a murky one. Whilst nations are attempting to curb the exploitation of IP and to teach their residents, the idea is catching on handiest slowly. Many growing countries face an investment crisis with regards to developing applications on IP attention.

Universities and is the time of many modifications for the higher. But first and predominant, it's far awareness time of the significance of intellectual property for improvement and boom on all tiers. It is the time to observe the records and act for that reason so one can carry Romania into the top ranks associated with competitiveness. In a globalized global, universities are visible increasingly as manufacturers of understanding, innovation, era, and qualified teams of workers from a strictly monetary point of view, accordingly contributing to the advent of wealth and competitive gain. It is also predicted that universities generate revenue due to the high demand for superior training that comes from everywhere in the international. But this should be checked out additionally thru the truth that universities do now not just produce technology and manpower, however, they shape humans, people, and an energetic part of society. For this reason, universities must create specialists who contribute to the long-time period countrywide well-being. The college is a valuable element in the generation of new ideas to persuade society. As a consequence, universities are required to recognize the need for issues and research that evaluate the effect of the latest expertise. This technique requires the integration of a take-a look at software focused on highbrow belongings which represents a primary step in growing a company aware of the electricity of innovation, knowledge, and intangible sources. The colleges can create an entrepreneurial culture and a subculture of innovation especially, they can promote innovation as an approach for lengthy-time period achievement and might make sure competitiveness in a generation ruled by way of globalization.

www.ingramcontent.com/pod-product-compliance
Lightning Source LLC
Chambersburg PA
CBHW051455150726
48000CB00005B/2400